Neil Armstrong

Jennifer Strand

abdopublishing.com

Published by Abdo Zoom™, PO Box 398166, Minneapolis, Minnesota 55439. Copyright © 2017 by Abdo Consulting Group, Inc. International copyrights reserved in all countries. No part of this book may be reproduced in any form without written permission from the publisher. Abdo Zoom™ is a trademark and logo of Abdo Consulting Group, Inc.

Printed in the United States of America, North Mankato, Minnesota
072016
092016

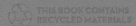

Cover Photo: NASA
Interior Photos: NASA, 1, 4, 4–5, 8, 10–11, 11, 12, 14, 15, 16, 17; Seth Poppel/Yearbook Library, 6; Shutterstock Images, 7; Everett Historical/Shutterstock Images, 9; NASA/AP Images, 18; Chris Stewart/ The Dayton Daily News/AP Images, 19

Editor: Emily Temple
Series Designer: Madeline Berger
Art Direction: Dorothy Toth

Publisher's Cataloging-in-Publication Data
Names: Strand, Jennifer, author.
Title: Neil Armstrong / by Jennifer Strand.
Description: Minneapolis, MN : Abdo Zoom, [2017] | Series: Pioneering
    explorers | Includes bibliographical references and index.
Identifiers: LCCN 2016941531 | ISBN 9781680792461 (lib. bdg.) |
    ISBN 9781680794144 (ebook) | 9781680795035 (Read-to-me ebook)
Subjects: LCSH: Armstrong, Neil,1932-2012--Juvenile literature. | Astronauts--
    United States--Biography--Juvenile literature. | Project Apollo (U.S.)--
    Juvenile literature. | Space flight to the moon--Juvenile literature.
Classification: DDC 629.45/0092 [B]--dc23
LC record available at http://lccn.loc.gov/2016941531

Table of Contents

Introduction

Neil Armstrong was an **astronaut**.

He was the first person to walk on the moon.

Early Life

Neil was born on August 5, 1930. He grew up in Ohio.

Neil read books about flying as a boy. He built model airplanes.

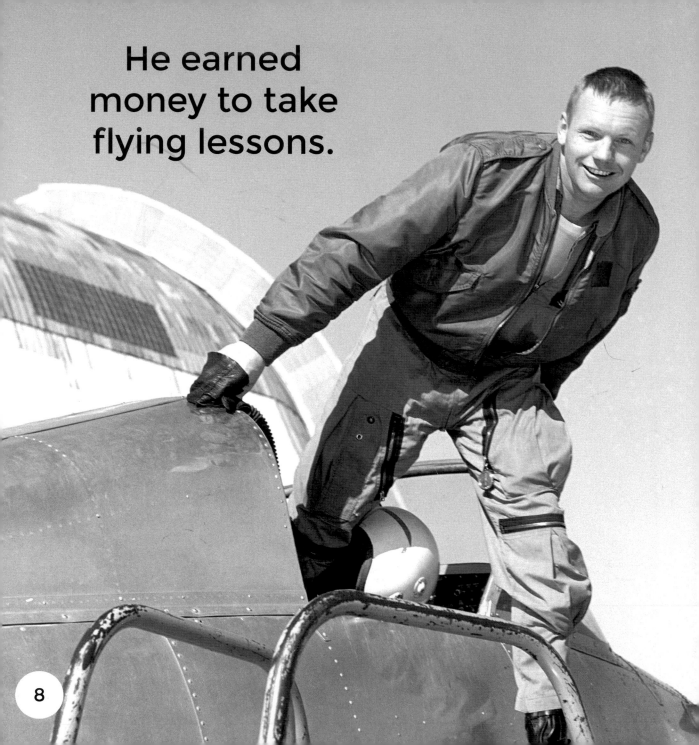

He earned
money to take
flying lessons.

After high school he **enlisted** in
the US Navy. He became a **pilot**.
He flew a plane in a war.

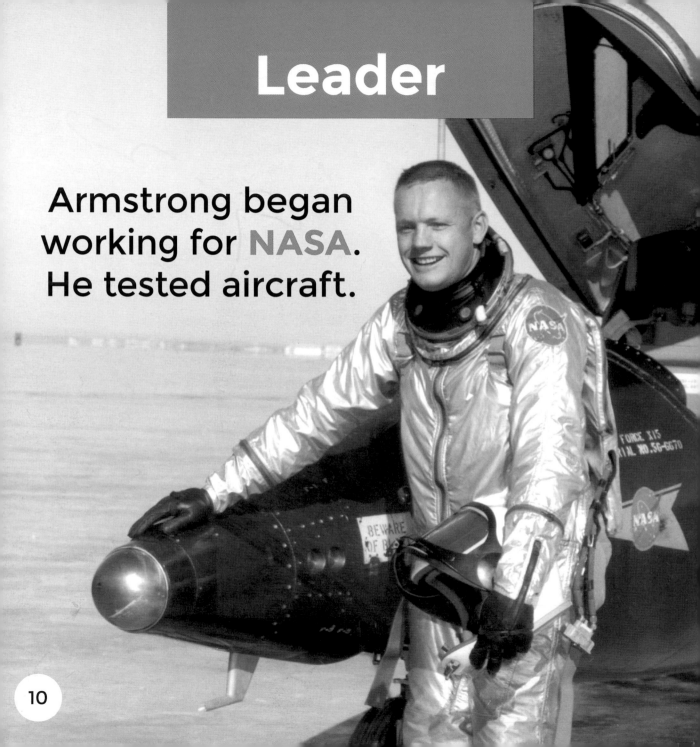

Leader

Armstrong began working for **NASA**. He tested aircraft.

Then he got into
the astronaut program.

NASA sent missions to space. The missions prepared for landing on the moon. They were called the Gemini and Apollo missions.

Armstrong went on a mission.
It was called Apollo 11.

His spacecraft landed on the moon.

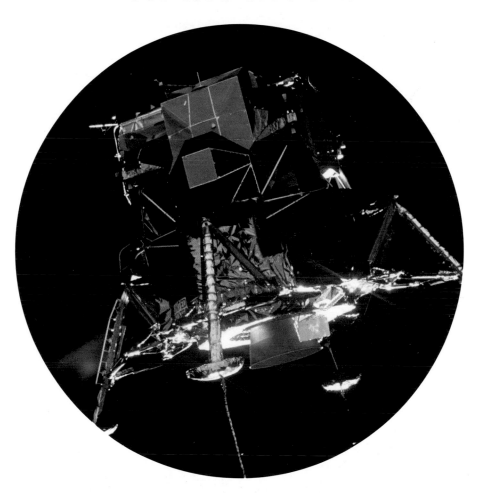

A few hours later Armstrong stepped outside.

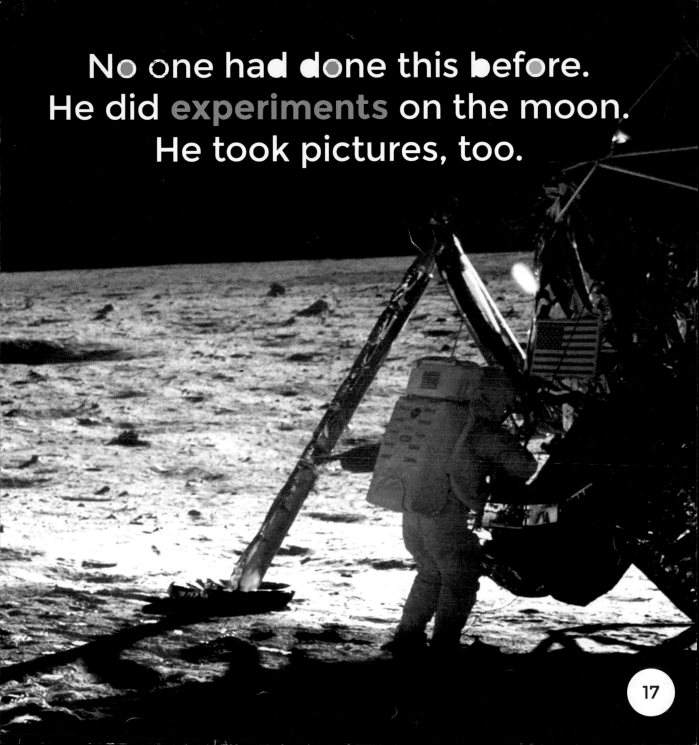

No one had done this before.
He did **experiments** on the moon.
He took pictures, too.

Legacy

Armstrong's work was important. He made history. In 1971 he left NASA.

He died on August 25, 2012.

Neil Armstrong

Born: August 5, 1930

Birthplace: Wapakoneta, Ohio

Wives: Janet Shearon (divorced); Carol Held Knight

Known For: Armstrong was an astronaut. He was the first person to walk on the moon.

Died: August 25, 2012

Key  Dates

1930: Neil Alden Armstrong is born on August 5.

1947: Armstrong joins the US Navy.

1966: Armstrong goes on his first space mission.

1969: Armstrong becomes the first person to walk on the moon on July 20.

1971: Armstrong retires from NASA. He becomes a college professor.

2012: Armstrong dies on August 25.

Glossary

astronaut - someone who travels to outer space.

enlisted - joined the army, navy, or one of the other armed forces.

experiment - a scientific test.

NASA - stands for National Aeronautics and Space Administration. It leads space exploration for the United States.

pilot - a person who flies an airplane or guides a ship.

Booklinks

For more information
on **Neil Armstrong**, please visit
booklinks.abdopublishing.com

Learn even more with the Abdo Zoom
Biographies database. Check out
abdozoom.com for more information.

Index

airplanes, 7

Apollo, 13, 14

born, 6

died, 19

Gemini, 13

missions, 13, 14

moon, 5, 13, 15, 17

NASA, 10, 13, 18

Ohio, 6

spacecraft, 15

US Navy, 9

war, 9